Sports Illustrated KIDS

SIDE BY SIDE

BASKETBALL STARS

Comparing Pro Basketball's Greatest Players

BY CHRISTOPHER FOREST

CAPSTONE PRESS
a capstone imprint

SIDE-BY-SIDE BASKETBALL STARS:
Comparing Pro Basketball's Greatest Players

For decades the National Basketball Association (NBA) has wowed the world with its amazing athletes. From Oscar Robertson and Elgin Baylor to Dr. J and Michael Jordan, each era has featured basketball superstars. In the 1980s the NBA showcased Magic Johnson against Larry Bird— one of the most intense player matchups of all time. Today high-scoring superstars such as Kevin Durant and Carmelo Anthony pile up the points all season long.

Whether comparing today's superstars or players across eras, it's fun to discuss which athletes would come out on top. Who would win a one-on-one matchup between LeBron James and Michael Jordan? Which big man would dominate the paint between Shaq and Tim Duncan? Check out the stats and then decide for yourself who would win these superstar matchups.

*All stats are through the 2013–14 regular season.

Sports Illustrated Kids Side-By-Side Sports are published by Capstone Press, 1710 Roe Crest Drive, North Mankato, Minnesota 56003 www.capstonepub.com

Printed in the United States of America in Stevens Point, Wisconsin.
032014   008092WZF14

TABLE OF CONTENTS

MICHAEL JORDAN VS. LEBRON JAMES 4

KOBE BRYANT VS. JERRY WEST 8

SHAQUILLE O'NEAL VS. TIM DUNCAN 12

KYRIE IRVING VS. RICKY RUBIO 16

RAY ALLEN VS. STEPHEN CURRY 20

CHRIS PAUL VS. TONY PARKER 24

JAMES HARDEN VS. DWYANE WADE 28

LARRY BIRD VS. EARVIN JOHNSON 32

KEVIN DURANT VS. CARMELO ANTHONY 36

BLAKE GRIFFIN VS. VINCE CARTER 40

Coach's Call 44

Critical Thinking Using the Common Core 46

Quotation Sources 46

Read More 47

Internet Sites 47

Index 48

MICHAEL
JORDAN

NICKNAME: Air Jordan
HEIGHT: 6 feet, 6 inches (198 cm)
WEIGHT: 195 pounds (88.5 kg)
YEARS ACTIVE: 1984–1993, 1994–1998, 2001–2003
TEAMS: Bulls, Wizards
CHAMPIONSHIPS: 6
ALL-STAR GAMES: 14
OLYMPICS: 2 gold
MVP AWARDS: 5
FINALS MVP AWARDS: 6
-Led league in scoring 11 times
-Holds the playoff record for most points in a
    game with 63
-Entered the Hall of Fame in 2009

Points	PPG	Rebounds	RPG	Assists	APG
32,292	30.1	6,672	6.2	5,633	5.3

4

LEBRON JAMES

NICKNAME: The King
HEIGHT: 6 feet, 8 inches (203 cm)
WEIGHT: 240 pounds (108.9 kg)
YEARS ACTIVE: 2003–present*
TEAMS: Cavaliers, Heat
CHAMPIONSHIPS: 1
ALL-STAR GAMES: 10
OLYMPICS: 2 gold, 1 bronze
MVP AWARDS: 4
FINALS MVP AWARDS: 2
-Led league in scoring once
-Had back-to-back triple doubles in the 2007 and 2008
  All-Star Games

Points	PPG	Rebounds	RPG	Assists	APG
23,170	27.5	6,086	7.2	5,790	6.9

*Stats are through the 2013–14 regular season.

"There's Michael Jordan and then there is the rest of us." —*Former Lakers guard Magic Johnson*

"Michael was doing so much and so well, I found myself just wanting to stop and watch him—and I was playing." —*Former teammate John Paxson on Jordan's 63-point performance in the 1986 playoffs*

Many basketball fans consider Michael Jordan to be the greatest player of all time. He is the third all-time leading scorer in the NBA and helped popularize the slam dunk contest. His success started in high school and carried into college, where he played for the University of North Carolina. As a freshman, he hit a game-winning shot in the 1982 NCAA championship basketball

game. The Chicago Bulls selected Jordan with the third pick in the 1984 draft. His speed and ability to soar to the basket caused fans to dub him "His Airness."

He quickly displayed his scoring ability at the professional level and was an All-Star starter in 1985. Jordan led the league in scoring in 1987 with 3,041 points, which ranks third on the all-time single-season list. But he was just warming up. He led the NBA in scoring for seven straight years and finished his career having led the NBA in points per game 10 times. Jordan was also a clutch performer in the playoffs. He raised the NBA championship trophy six times, all with the Chicago Bulls.

LEBRON JAMES

LeBron James was destined for stardom since he was a teenager. As a freshman at St. Vincent-St. Mary High School in Akron, Ohio, he led his team to the Division III State Championship. By the end of high school, he was ready for the NBA. The Cleveland Cavaliers made James the first pick in the 2003 draft. He earned the Rookie of the Year award after the 2003–04 season, averaging 20.9 points per game. During the 2005–06 season, James became the youngest MVP of an All-Star Game. He led the Cavs to the NBA Finals in 2007, but they lost to the San Antonio Spurs.

In 2010 James made the decision to sign with the Miami Heat. In his first year with his new team, the Heat lost to the Dallas Mavericks in the NBA Finals. But in 2012 James led the Heat to a championship victory over the Oklahoma City Thunder and was named the Finals MVP. The following year, James earned his second Finals MVP as the Heat celebrated a championship win over the San Antonio Spurs. James continued to put up big numbers in 2014, scoring a career-high and franchise-record 61 points in a game against the Charlotte Bobcats.

"Over these 46 years, I've had an opportunity to see some great players. … In my humble opinion, I believe the man right here is the best of them all." —*Miami Heat general manager Pat Riley*

"He's not intimidated by anyone. He has that swagger that most of the great ones have."
—*Former Cleveland Cavaliers coach Paul Silas*

KOBE BRYANT

NICKNAME: The Black Mamba
HEIGHT: 6 feet, 7 inches (201 cm)
WEIGHT: 200 pounds (90.7 kg)
YEARS ACTIVE: 1996–present*
TEAM: Lakers
CHAMPIONSHIPS: 5
ALL-STAR GAMES: 15
MVP AWARDS: 1
FINALS MVP AWARDS: 2
-All-time leading scorer in Lakers history
-Led the NBA in scoring four times

Points	PPG	Rebounds	RPG	Assists	APG
31,700	25.5	6,601	5.3	5,925	4.8

*Stats are through the 2013–14 regular season.

JERRY WEST

NICKNAME: Mr. Clutch
HEIGHT: 6 feet, 2 inches (188 cm)
WEIGHT: 175 pounds (79.4 kg)
YEARS ACTIVE: 1960–1974
TEAM: Lakers
CHAMPIONSHIPS: 1
ALL-STAR GAMES: 14
FINALS MVP AWARDS: 1
-*Second all-time leading scorer in Lakers history*
-*Entered the Hall of Fame in 1980*

Points	PPG	Rebounds	RPG	Assists	APG
25,192	27.0	5,366	5.8	6,238	6.7

KOBE BRYANT

Basketball is in Kobe Bryant's blood. His father, Joe, played on several NBA and European teams, so it was natural that Kobe followed in his footsteps. He was a high school superstar, averaging 30.8 points a game in 1996. After high school, Kobe opted to enter the 1996 NBA draft. He was selected by the Charlotte Hornets in 1996 but was traded to the Los Angeles Lakers.

By his third year, Bryant was a force on the court, leading the Lakers to the first of three straight championships. His ability to score was put on display in 2006, when he hauled in 81 points in a single game. He ranks fourth all-time on the scoring list, and he is closing in fast on Michael Jordan's total. Bryant also has a knack for clutch shooting, connecting on 28 game-winning shots. His speed and ability to affect the outcome of a game have made him one of the game's greatest players.

"What he has accomplished with this team, I don't think there's any question in my mind at this point in time—because of him being with this team for his whole career—that he has been the greatest Laker player."
—Jerry West

"He's the best player in basketball. I don't think it's even close." —NBA coach Alvin Gentry

Jerry West was a basketball star long before becoming Mr. Clutch for the Los Angeles Lakers. As a senior in high school, he averaged 32 points a game and led his team to the 1956 state championship. He played college hoops at West Virginia University and led the team to the 1959 NCAA championship. In 1960 West began playing for the Lakers, taking the team to the Finals nine times in 14 seasons. West averaged an eye-popping 40.6 points a game in the 1965 playoffs.

In 1969 the Lakers squared off against the Boston Celtics in the NBA Finals but lost in seven games. After averaging 37.9 points and 7.4 assists in the championship series, West became the only Finals MVP to come from the losing team. The following year, he led the league in scoring with 31.2 points per game. He finally earned a championship ring in 1972, as the Lakers beat the Milwaukee Bucks in the Finals. When he finished his career in 1974, most people believed he was one of the greatest shooters ever to play the game.

"He taught me about what greatness was. I could see this pressure and will to perform night in and night out."

—Former teammate and Lakers coach Pat Riley

"I never played the game with anyone who played as hard." —Former teammate and Laker guard Elgin Baylor

SHAQUILLE
O'NEAL

NICKNAME: Shaq
HEIGHT: 7 feet, 1 inch (216 cm)
WEIGHT: 325 pounds (147.4 kg)
YEARS ACTIVE: 1992–2011
TEAMS: Magic, Lakers, Heat, Suns, Cavaliers, Celtics
CHAMPIONSHIPS: 4
ALL-STAR GAMES: 15
OLYMPICS: 1 gold
MVP AWARDS: 1
FINALS MVP AWARDS: 3
–Led the NBA in scoring twice
–Named MVP of the All-Star Game three times

Points	PPG	Rebounds	RPG	Blocks	BPG
28,596	23.7	13,099	10.9	2,732	2.3

TIM DUNCAN

NICKNAME: The Big Fundamental
HEIGHT: 6 feet, 11 inches (211 cm)
WEIGHT: 248 pounds (112.5 kg)
YEARS ACTIVE: 1997–present*
TEAM: Spurs
CHAMPIONSHIPS: 4
ALL-STAR GAMES: 14
OLYMPICS: 1 bronze
MVP AWARDS: 2
FINALS MVP AWARDS: 3
-Only the second player to earn MVP honors in his
    first three trips to the NBA Finals
-Named 1997–98 Rookie of the Year

Points	PPG	Rebounds	RPG	Blocks	BPG
24,904	19.9	13,940	11.1	2,791	2.2

SHAQUILLE O'NEAL

From a young age, Shaquille O'Neal knew how to use his size to dominate the post on the basketball court. He averaged 32 points and 22 rebounds as a high school senior, leading his team to a Texas state championship. After high school, O'Neal took his skills to Louisiana

State University, blocking a record 11 shots in a single game in the 1992 NCAA tournament. Shaq entered the NBA draft that year, and the Orlando Magic picked him first overall.

As an NBA rookie, he netted 23 points per game. Two years later, he led the league in scoring while guiding the Magic to the NBA Finals. O'Neal signed with the Los Angeles Lakers in 1996 and continued to dominate the paint. He was voted league MVP in the third year with his new team. Behind Shaq's MVP play, the Lakers went all the way in the NBA Finals that year—the first of three straight championships. In 2004 Shaq was traded to the Miami Heat, where he earned yet another championship ring.

"This is a guy who could and should have been the MVP player for 10 consecutive seasons."
—*Former Lakers coach Phil Jackson*

"I always thought as a player when they asked me who the hardest player was to go against, it was him. His size, his strength, his power."
—*Forward Pau Gasol*

"He sees the court as well or better than a lot of guards. When I look at him I see nothing but greatness." —*Hall of Famer Jerry West*

"He gets the job done, night in and night out. He's versatile, totally able to do the things his team needs him to do to win."
—*Former NBA star Kareem Abdul-Jabbar*

Tim Duncan is sometimes called the quiet man in the lane, but his play speaks for itself. He honed his skills playing college basketball for Wake Forest University, winning Player of the Year in 1997. That year, the San Antonio Spurs selected Duncan with the first pick in the draft. He paired with center David Robinson to pose a tremendous force in the paint.

The following year, Duncan helped lead the Spurs to the 1999 NBA Championship. He netted 22 points in the 2000 All-Star Game, earning co-MVP status with Shaquille O'Neal. In 2002 he earned the first of two consecutive league MVP awards, averaging 25.5 points and 12.7 rebounds a game. His smooth moves near the hoop lifted the Spurs to championships in 2003, 2005, and 2007. A beast around the boards, Duncan has reached the top five in rebounding in 10 seasons. After the 2013–14 season, he held the 11th spot on the all-time rebounding list. There is no doubt that Duncan will be remembered as one of the strongest post players of all time.

KYRIE
IRVING

NICKNAME: Uncle Drew
HEIGHT: 6 feet, 2 inches (188 cm)
WEIGHT: 180 (81.6 kg)
YEARS ACTIVE: 2011–present*
TEAM: Cavaliers
ALL-STAR GAMES: 2
2012 ROOKIE OF THE YEAR

Points	PPG	Assists	APG	Steals	SPG
3,747	20.7	1,058	5.8	251	1.4

RICKY RUBIO

NICKNAME: La Pistola
HEIGHT: 6 feet, 4 inches (193 cm)
WEIGHT: 180 pounds (81.6 kg)
YEARS ACTIVE: 2011–present*
TEAM: Timberwolves
OLYMPIC MEDALS: 1 silver (for Spain)
-Finished second to Kyrie Irving in 2012
    Rookie of the Year voting

Points	PPG	Assists	APG	Steals	SPG
1,825	10.1	1,458	8.1	419	2.3

KYRIE IRVING

Kyrie Irving is a young legend in the making. As a senior in high school, Irving was an All-American and the New Jersey player of the year. He enrolled at Duke University in 2010 and continued to play ball. In the season opener, he set Duke's freshman single-game record with nine assists.

Irving entered the NBA draft in 2011 and was picked first overall by the Cleveland Cavaliers. He averaged 18.5 points and 5.4 assists in the lockout-shortened NBA season that year and was named NBA Rookie of the Year. He improved the following year, averaging 22.5 points per game. In just his third season, Irving was named the MVP of the All-Star Game by scoring 31 points and tallying 14 assists. As his game continues to grow, there is no doubt Irving is a superstar point guard on the rise.

"Kyrie is doing it all ... He's so explosive."
—*NBA legend Magic Johnson*

"He's already unbelievable in this league. ... What he's doing right now, and what he's going to do in the future, it's going to be crazy."
—*Miami Heat forward LeBron James*

Ricky Rubio's speed and passing ability gained attention when he made his Spanish ACB League at age 14. By his third season in the league, he was scoring double digits on a regular basis. In 2009 the Minnesota Timberwolves selected him with the fifth overall pick in the NBA draft. Rubio remained in Europe in 2010–11 and guided his team to his first ACB League championship.

With a championship season under his belt, Rubio jumped to the NBA, joining the Timberwolves in 2011. He averaged 10.6 points and 8.2 assists in 41 games his rookie year, but his season ended after he tore ligaments in his knee. The following year, he bounced back and continued to showcase his unique style of shooting and passing. He led the league with 191 steals in 2013–14 while averaging a career high 8.6 assists per game. With his ability to make difficult passes, score quickly, and defend, Rubio will be a guard to reckon with for years to come.

"Rubio creates a shot. He's got instincts, great instincts." —*NBA legend Magic Johnson*

"He's very fun to play with and the type of player who you have to be ready at all times, because that ball is coming at you from any angle." —*Teammate Kevin Love*

RAY
ALLEN

NICKNAME: Sugar Ray
HEIGHT: 6 feet, 5 inches (196 cm)
WEIGHT: 205 pounds (93 kg)
YEARS ACTIVE: 1996–present*
TEAMS: Bucks, SuperSonics, Celtics, Heat
CHAMPIONSHIPS: 2
ALL-STAR GAMES: 10
OLYMPIC MEDALS: 1 gold
-All-time NBA leader in three-pointers

Points	PPG	3-Pointers	3-Pointers/Game	Career 3-Pointer %
24,505	18.9	2,973	2.3	40.0

*Stats are through the 2013–14 regular season.

STEPHEN
CURRY

NICKNAME: Baby-Faced Assassin
HEIGHT: 6 feet, 3 inches (191 cm)
WEIGHT: 185 pounds (83.9 kg)
YEARS ACTIVE: 2009–present*
TEAM: Warriors
ALL-STAR GAMES: 1
INTERNATIONAL MEDALS: 2010 Gold Medal at
   FIBA World Championship
-Set the single-season record for three-pointers (272)

Points	PPG	3-Pointers	3-Pointers/Game	Career 3-Pointer %

RAY ALLEN

"Ray is hands down the best shooter in NBA history. ... Every time he gets the ball we think it's going in."
—Former teammate Nate Robinson

"He's not only the best player I've ever coached, he's one of the best people I've ever been involved with." —Former University of Connecticut coach Jim Calhoun

Ray Allen is known throughout the NBA for his smooth stroke behind the three-point line. When he was a senior in high school, he led his team to the state championship. As a junior at the University of Connecticut, Allen averaged 23.4 points per game. The Minnesota Timberwolves selected him with the fifth overall pick in the NBA draft and traded him to the Milwaukee Bucks. He quickly became known for his keen outside shot and strong free throw shooting. Allen was traded to the Seattle SuperSonics during the 2002–03 season. He averaged more than 20 points per game over five seasons in Seattle. During that stretch, he set a record by hitting 269 three-pointers in a single season.

He was traded to the Boston Celtics in 2007, where he paired up with Paul Pierce and Kevin Garnett. The Big Three won 66 games that year, and Allen won his first NBA championship. As a Celtic, he passed Reggie Miller for the most three-pointers made in NBA history. Following the 2011–12 season, Allen brought his lethal outside shot to the Miami Heat, where he won his second NBA championship. With each season that passes, Allen continues to distance himself as the top three-point shooter in NBA history.

STEPHEN CURRY

Stephen Curry has made a name for himself for his smooth outside shot and quick hands. As a sophomore at Davidson College, he set the single-season NCAA record for three-pointers with 162. As a junior, he led the entire nation in scoring with 28.6 points per game.

Following his junior year, Curry entered the 2009 NBA draft and was chosen with the seventh overall pick by the Golden State Warriors. He averaged 17.5 points per game in his first season and hit 166 three-pointers—a rookie record. In his second year, Curry scored 272 three pointers, breaking Ray Allen's single-season record. His points per game jumped to 24.0 in 2013–14, and he averaged 8.5 assists—both career highs. It's no surprise he again led the NBA in three-pointers, netting 261 threes and claiming the fourth spot on the all-time single-season list. Curry has proven to be one of the NBA's greatest shooters in the game today.

"When's he's open, I always feel like the ball is going in. He's got that gift."
—Former Warriors guard Chris Mullin

"He's the best shooter in our league."
—NBA coach Doc Rivers

CHRIS PAUL

NICKNAME: CP3
HEIGHT: 6 feet (183 cm)
WEIGHT: 175 pounds (79.4 kg)
YEARS ACTIVE: 2005–present*
TEAMS: Hornets, Clippers
ALL-STAR GAMES: 6
OLYMPIC MEDALS: 2 gold, 1 bronze
2006 NBA ROOKIE OF THE YEAR
-Led NBA in assists twice
-Led NBA in steals five times

Points	PPG	Assists	APG	Steals	SPG
11,496	18.6	6,112	9.9	1,485	*2.4

TONY
PARKER

NICKNAME: Parisian Torpedo
HEIGHT: 6 feet, 2 inches (188 cm)
WEIGHT: 180 pounds (81.6 kg)
YEARS ACTIVE: 2001–present*
TEAM: Spurs
CHAMPIONSHIPS: 3
ALL-STAR GAMES: 5
FINALS MVP AWARDS: 1

-*Appeared in more playoff games (80) before he was
   24 than any other player in NBA history*
-*Franchise leader in assists*

Points	PPG	Assists	APG	Steals	SPG
16,051	17.1	5,635	6.0	872	0.9

*Stats are through the 2013–14 regular season.

CHRIS PAUL

Chris Paul controls the basketball court with a strong ability to pass the ball and play defense. He played for the West Forsyth varsity team in North Carolina his junior and senior year in high school. As a senior in 2002–03, he scored 30 points per game and was voted North Carolina's Mr. Basketball. The following year, he played NCAA basketball for Wake Forest University and was named ACC Rookie of the Year.

In 2005 Paul became the fourth pick in the NBA draft by the New Orleans Hornets. He got off to a fast start, showing his quick hands on the court by leading the league in steals during his rookie season. In 2007–08 Chris guided the Hornets to 56 victories— second best in the NBA. He was also named to his first All-Star Game that year, where he scored 16 points and added 14 assists. In 2011 Paul brought his ball-hawking skills to the Clippers, helping transform the team into a Western Conference power. He continued his dominance in 2013–14 by leading the NBA with 10.7 assists and 2.5 steals per game. With a deadly combination of scoring, passing, and defense, Paul is an all-around superstar.

"He has an uncanny way of getting the ball to you. That's something you're born with, a special trait that's inside of you."
—*Former Hornets teammate P.J. Brown*

"He's a general. He wins. He's a warrior, and he's going to take this whole organization to the next level." —*Clippers general manager Neil Olshey*

Tony Parker's love of basketball began at an early age, while watching his father play in Europe. It's no surprise that he started playing professionally in France when he was 15. Four years later, he entered the NBA draft and was selected by the San Antonio Spurs. He hit the court running his first season, earning All-Rookie Team honors. In 2002–03—just his second year in the NBA—he netted 15.5 points per game and helped the Spurs to an NBA title.

The Spurs won the title again in 2004–05, with Parker scoring 17.2 points in the playoffs. But he was just warming up. During the 2005–06 season, Parker's play earned him his first All-Star selection. He won another championship in 2006–07, averaging 20.8 points and 5.8 assists in the playoffs and earning the Finals MVP award. With great ball-handling skills and a keen ability to see the floor, Parker is one of the most feared guards in the NBA.

"He runs the pick-and-roll really well, [and] he knows when to push the ball and when to slow it down and settle the offense."

—*Former Spurs teammate Terry Porter*

"He's aggressive and he has no fear."

—*Spurs Coach Greg Popovich*

AMES HARDEN

NICKNAME: The Beard

HEIGHT: 6 feet, 5 inches (196 cm)

WEIGHT: 220 pounds (9.8 kg)

YEARS ACTIVE: 2009–present*

TEAMS: Thunder, Rockets

ALL-STAR GAMES: 1

2011-12 SIXTH MAN OF THE YEAR

OLYMPICS: 1 gold

-*In 2011 he scored a game-high 30 points in the NBA Rookie Challenge during the All-Star Weekend*

Points	PPG	Assists	APG	Steals	SPG
6,669	18.0	1,443	3.9	491	1.3

DWYANE WADE

NICKNAME: D-Wade
HEIGHT: 6 feet, 4 inches (193 cm)
WEIGHT: 212 pounds (96.2 kg)
YEARS ACTIVE: 2003–present*
TEAM: Heat
ALL-STAR GAMES: 9
NBA CHAMPIONSHIPS: 3
FINALS MVP AWARDS: 1
OLYMPICS: 1 bronze
-Led the NBA in scoring once

Points	PPG	Assists	APG	Steals	SPG
17,481	24.3	4,301	6.0	1,262	1.8

JAMES HARDEN

James Harden has become known for his scoring ability and aggressive style of play. He played basketball at Artesia High School in Lakewood, California. He averaged more than 18 points per game in his last two seasons of high school and won consecutive state championships. After high school, Harden played for Arizona State University and averaged 17.8 points per game.

The following year he was named Pac-10 Player of the Year.

Harden joined the Oklahoma City Thunder as the third overall pick in the 2009 draft. In his second year, he won the Sixth Man of the Year award and netted 16.8 points per game. In 2012 he was traded to the Houston Rockets, where he became a starter and truly began to shine. He averaged 25.9 points in 2012–13 and 25.4 points per game in 2013–14, making the All-Star team both years. Harden's hard-nosed approach, pesky defense, and ability to find the basket ensure that he'll be a star for years to come.

"He's an elite offensive player, a complete player." —*Rockets general manager Daryl Morey*

"He's a terrific player. He's an All-Star player. He's definitely at that level, and he's going to be that way for many, many, many years. "
—*Oklahoma City Thunder coach Scott Brooks*

Dwyane Wade has earned a reputation as a clutch performer and unstoppable scorer. He showed his scoring abilities as a high school senior, averaging 27 points and 11 rebounds. Wade netted 21.5 points per game as a junior for Marquette University and helped lead a charge to the 2003 Final Four. Later that year, Wade was drafted by the Miami Heat

with the fifth pick. As a rookie in 2003–04, he scored 16.2 points per game. Two years later, Wade averaged 27.4 points and 7.5 assists while driving the Heat to its first NBA championship.

Wade led the league in scoring in 2008–09, averaging an incredible 30.2 points per game. In the 2010 All-Star Game, he was named MVP after scoring 28 points and dishing out 11 assists. Wade added two more championships to his achievements as the Heat won back-to-back championships in 2012 and 2013. Earning his 10th straight All-Star appearance in 2013–14, he continues to prove that he is one of the greatest all-around players in the game.

"There are lots of guys in this league who can get to the rim, but Dwyane has the strength to finish." —*Former NBA coach Bernie Bickerstaff*

"His unselfishness and understanding of the team concept are what makes him great."
—*Miami Heat general manager Pat Riley*

LARRY BIRD

NICKNAME: Larry Legend
HEIGHT: 6 feet, 9 inches (206 cm)
WEIGHT: 220 pounds (99.8 kg)
YEARS ACTIVE: 1979–1992
TEAM: Celtics
CHAMPIONSHIPS: 3
ALL-STAR GAMES: 12
MVP AWARDS: 3
FINALS MVP AWARDS: 2
OLYMPICS: 1 gold
-Won the first ever three-point shooting contest at the 1986 NBA All-Star Game
-Entered the Hall of Fame in 1998

Points	PPG	Rebounds	RPG	Assists	APG
21,791	24.3	8,974	10.0	5,695	6.3

EARVIN
JOHNSON

NICKNAME: Magic

HEIGHT: 6 feet, 9 inches (206 cm)

WEIGHT: 215 pounds (97.5 kg)

YEARS ACTIVE: 1979–1991, 1995–1996

TEAM: Lakers

CHAMPIONSHIPS: 5

ALL-STAR GAMES: 12

MVP AWARDS: 3

FINALS MVP AWARDS: 3

OLYMPICS: 1 gold

-First rookie to earn a Finals MVP award

-Entered the Hall of Fame in 2002

Points	PPG	Rebounds	RPG	Assists	APG
17,707	19.5	6,559	7.2	10,141	11.2

Larry Bird helped make the NBA popular in the 1980s with his slick passes, heads-up play, and lights-out shooting. His success started at a young age with his Springs Valley High School team in Indiana. Averaging 31 points his senior year, Bird became the school's all-time leading scorer. At the college level, Bird played for little-known Indiana State University. As a senior, he led his team to its first NCAA tournament. The Sycamores battled all the way to the NCAA Finals before losing to Magic Johnson and Michigan State.

The rivalry continued in the NBA, as Bird joined the Boston Celtics in 1979 and narrowly beat out Johnson for Rookie of the Year. Bird propelled the Celtics to their 14th NBA championship one year later, scoring 21.2 points per game. In the 1983–84 season, Bird won the first of three consecutive league MVP awards while guiding the Celtics to another championship. In 1986 he captained what some fans consider to be the best NBA team ever to a 67-win season and his third championship. He retired in 1992 as one of the greatest players to ever take the court.

"On the court, Larry was the only player I feared and he was the smartest player I ever played against." —*Magic Johnson*

"Any living legend can take over a game in the last few minutes. Only Bird can take it over in the first few minutes." —*Sportswriter Peter Vescey*

MAGIC JOHNSON

Earvin "Magic" Johnson first gained attention for his brilliant passes and athleticism at Everett High School in Michigan. As a senior, he guided his team to a state championship. He went on to play basketball in college at nearby Michigan State. As a sophomore, he led his team to the 1979 NCAA Finals and beat Larry Bird's Indiana State Sycamores.

A year later, Johnson was selected first overall by the Los Angeles Lakers in the NBA draft. In his rookie year, he helped the Lakers win the 1980 NBA championship. He earned the Finals MVP and showed his versatility by playing all five positions in the series. Magic won four more titles and earned three league MVP trophies in his career. The 12-time All-Star led the league in assists three times. He piled up 10,141 assists in his career, which places him fifth on the all-time list. He is remembered as one of the NBA's greatest players, and his ability to pass the ball still seems like magic today.

"Magic is head and shoulders above everyone else." —*Larry Bird*

"He's the only player who can take only three shots and still dominate a game."
—*Former NBA star Julius Erving*

KEVIN DURANT

NICKNAME: Durantula
HEIGHT: 6 feet, 9 inches (206 cm)
WEIGHT: 215 pounds (97.5 kg)
YEARS ACTIVE: 2007–present*
TEAM: Thunder
ALL-STAR GAMES: 4
MVP AWARDS: 1
OLYMPICS: 1 gold
2007-08 ROOKIE OF THE YEAR
-Led the NBA in scoring five times

Points	PPG	Rebounds	RPG	Assists	APG
14,851	27.4	3,751	6.9	1,892	3.5

CARMELO
ANTHONY

NICKNAME: Melo
HEIGHT: 6 feet, 8 inches (203 cm)
WEIGHT: 230 pounds (104.3 kg)
YEARS ACTIVE: 2003–present*
TEAMS: Nuggets, Knicks
ALL-STAR GAMES: 6
OLYMPICS: 2 gold, 1 bronze
-Tied an NBA record by making 33 points in one
    quarter in 2008

Points	PPG	Rebounds	RPG	Assists	APG
19,958	25.3	5,173	6.5	2,423	3.1

Kevin Durant has an unusual combination of size and ability to knock down shots from anywhere on the court. He was a talented shooter in high school, scoring 23.6 points per game as a senior. As a freshman at the University of Texas, Durant scored 25.8 points per game and was named AP Player of the Year.

He was ready to enter the NBA the following year, and he was chosen second overall by the Seattle SuperSonics. He was a star right out of the gate, winning Rookie of the Year honors by pouring in 20.3 points per game. A year later, the team moved to Oklahoma City and became the Thunder. In 2009–10 Durant led the NBA in scoring and averaged 30.1 points per game. He was the 2012 league MVP and led the Thunder to the Finals. In 2013–14 he scored an amazing 2,593 points, leading the league for the fifth straight year. He reached career highs that season with averages of 32.0 points and 5.5 assists per game. With so much accomplished in only seven years in the NBA, Durant is primed for a remarkable career.

"He's got all the ability in the world, and he keeps getting better."

—*Former Minnesota Timberwolves coach Rick Adelman*

"The guy is nearly seven feet tall and comes off screens shooting like Ray Allen."
—*Miami Heat forward Shane Battier*

There are few players who can drain buckets like Carmelo Anthony. His scoring touch awed fans when he was a junior in high school. He was named the 2001–02 Baltimore City and County Player of the Year. Anthony attended Syracuse University in 2002 and led the Orangemen to a national championship. He averaged 22.2 points per game and was named the Final Four Most Outstanding Player.

Anthony joined the Denver Nuggets in 2003 and averaged 21 points per game as a rookie, finishing second to LeBron James in the Rookie of the Year voting. In the middle of his eighth season with the Nuggets, he was traded to the New York Knicks—the team he rooted for as a youth. He put on a scoring display in 2012–13 with a league-best 28.7 points per game. In 2013–14 he was named to his seventh All-Star Game, where he piled up 30 points and eight 3-pointers. Anthony continues to dazzle the crowd with his array of shots and ability to command the game.

"Carmelo's just a tremendous offensive force with a tremendous, versatile skill set and ability to score in bunches."

—*Former Knicks forward Bernard King*

"I don't think there's anybody, or any two guys, who can guard him if he's shooting the ball well." —*Syracuse University coach Jim Boeheim*

BLAKE
GRIFFIN

NICKNAME: High Griffinition
HEIGHT: 6 feet, 10 inches (208 cm)
WEIGHT: 251 pounds (113.9 kg)
YEARS ACTIVE: 2009–present*
TEAM: Clippers
ALL-STAR GAMES: 2
2010-11 ROOKIE OF THE YEAR
2011 SLAM DUNK CHAMPION
-Rookie of the month winner six times in his first season

Points	PPG	Rebounds	RPG	Assists	APG
6,583	21.4	3,125	10.1	1,130	3.7

VINCE CARTER

NICKNAME: Vinsanity
HEIGHT: 6 feet, 6 inches (198 cm)
WEIGHT: 220 pounds (99.8 kg)
YEARS ACTIVE: 1998–present*
TEAMS: Raptors, Nets, Magic, Suns, Mavericks
ALL-STAR GAMES: 8
1998-99 ROOKIE OF THE YEAR
2000 SLAM DUNK CHAMPION
-All-time leading scorer in Toronto Raptors history
  (9,420 points)

Points	PPG	Rebounds	RPG	Assists	APG
23,190	20.2	5,634	4.9	4,242	3.7

Blake Griffin brings raw strength and athleticism to the court day after day. His love of basketball came from his father and older brother. Griffin won four consecutive state championships with his high school team, which was coached by his dad. During his senior year, he averaged 26.8 points and 15.1 rebounds. Griffin played basketball for two years at Oklahoma University and was named College Player of the Year as a sophomore.

The Los Angeles Clippers made him the first overall draft pick in 2009, but he missed his rookie season after suffering an injury. He returned the following year with a boom, scoring 22.5 points and grabbing 12.1 rebounds per game. In 2011 Griffin wowed the crowd at the slam dunk contest by jumping over a car and slamming the ball through the hoop. His amazing dunk made him the champion and showed basketball fans what Griffin is capable of. In 2014 he tied Kevin Durant for most points scored in the All-Star Game with 38. He continues to evolve into a dominant player, and his legend grows with each thunderous slam.

"It's really an art form, the way he uses his body and craftiness."
—*Minnesota Timberwolves forward Kevin Love*

"I don't think we've ever seen a guy whose energy level is that high. The guy plays at an incredible rate." —*Former NBA coach Keith Smart*

Vince Carter is one of the NBA's greatest dunkers. He idolized NBA dunking legend Dr. J and slammed his own first dunk when he was 12. Carter played at Mainland High School in Daytona Beach and was selected as the Florida Player of the Year as a senior. He played college hoops for the University of North Carolina and averaged 12.3 points per game.

He debuted with the Toronto Raptors in 1998–99 and won Rookie of the Year honors while scoring 18.3 points per game. The following year, Carter won the 2000 NBA slam dunk contest. He displayed his athleticism by pulling off a reverse 360 on one dunk and putting his arm through the hoop up to his elbow on another. He even took a bounce pass and switched the ball from his left hand to his right hand between his legs before dunking it through the hoop. Carter was named to eight All-Star teams, but his claim to fame is his ability to slam the ball. In 2013 *Sports Illustrated* voted him the "number 1 dunker who rocked the world."

"Vince Carter is one of those guys who can take a quarter off the top of the backboard ... and put one back up there!"

—*Former NBA guard Allen Iverson*

"Watching Vince Carter is like going to a movie." —*Former NBA player Charles Oakley*

COACH'S CALL

Michael Jordan vs. LeBron James:

James may be the greatest player in the game today and may have more championships in his future. But Jordan led the Bulls to six championships and became an icon on the court. The nod goes to Jordan.

Michael Jordan

Kobe Bryant vs. Jerry West:

Jerry West was one of the greatest Lakers of all time, but Kobe has completely dominated the league at times. The vote goes to Kobe Bryant and his five championships.

Shaquille O'Neal vs. Tim Duncan:

Duncan has long been controlling the post for the Spurs and has three championships under his belt. But in his prime, O'Neal was an unstoppable force. For a big man under the hoop, I'll go with Shaq.

Kyrie Irving

Kyrie Irving vs. Ricky Rubio:

Rubio runs the point well and is a pickpocket on the court. But Irving is the driving force of his team and can outscore Rubio on a regular basis. The edge goes to Irving.

Ray Allen vs. Stephen Curry:

Curry is the best current sharpshooter and set the single-season record for 3-pointers. But Allen has proven his consistency and is the NBA's all-time three-point leader. Although Curry may surpass Allen one day, my choice is Allen.

Chris Paul vs. Tony Parker:

Parker can hit tough shots and knows how to control the tempo of the game. But Paul can pass, shoot, and score at will. This tough call goes to Paul.

James Harden vs. Dwyane Wade:

Harden is tough to beat around the basket and has come into his own with the Houston Rockets. However, Wade has been the league's top scorer and has won three championships. The vote goes to D-Wade.

Larry Bird vs. Magic Johnson:

Both players made the NBA popular with their classic matchup, and they are both legends of the game. Bird may have won three straight MVPs, but the edge goes to Magic and his five championships.

Dwayne Wade

Kevin Durant

Carmelo Anthony vs. Kevin Durant:

Anthony is consistently one of the top scorers in the game, but Durant has led the league in scoring five times. His 2,593 points in 2013–14 put him in the top 20 for single-season records, and he keeps getting better. I'll pick Durant—the 2014 MVP award winner—as my go-to scorer.

Blake Griffin vs. Vince Carter:

Carter helped popularize the slam dunk in the 1990s and early 2000s. But the pick goes to Blake Griffin, who makes backboards quiver nightly.

Critical Thinking Using the Common Core

1. Reread pages 16–19 and 24–27. Which point guard would you want bringing the ball up the court for your team? Support your choice with information from the text. (Key Ideas and Details)

2. Larry Bird and Magic Johnson are NBA legends who dominated the NBA in the 1980s. How do you think they would compare with today's players? Why? Support your answer with evidence from the text and from other books or online sources. (Integration of Knowledge and Ideas)

3. Look at the choices the author made on pages 44 and 45 of the Coach's Call section. Do you agree with the picks? Why or why not? Support your choices with information from this book, as well as from other books or online sources. (Integration of Knowledge and Ideas)

Quotation Sources

www.nba.com, 6a, 6b, 7a, 22a, 34b, 43a, 43b; www.jockbio.com, 7b, 10a, 15a, 15b, 22b, 27b, 30a, 31b, 38a, 38b, 39b, 42b; http://onemanfastbreak.net, 10b; http://blog.lakers.com, 11a, 11b, 14a; www.sportsnippets.com, 14b; www.cleveland.com/cavs, 18a; www.miamiherald.com, 18b; www.espn.go.com, 19a, 35b; www.sbnation.com, 19b; www.mercurynews.com, 23a; www.boston.com/sports, 23b; http://sportsillustrated.cnn.com, 26a, 27a, 31a, 42a; www.foxnews.com/sports, 26b; http://newsok.com, 30b; www.registerguard.com, 34a; www.suntimes.com, 35a; http://nypost.com, 39a

Read More

Aaseng, Nathan. *Michael Jordan: Hall of Fame Basketball Superstar.* Berkeley Heights, N.J.: Enslow Publishers, Inc., 2013.

Doeden, Matt. *Basketball Legends in the Making.* Sports Illustrated Kids. North Mankato, Minn.: Capstone Press, 2014.

Edwards, Ethan. *Meet Blake Griffin: Basketball's Slam Dunk King.* New York: PowerKids Press, 2014.

Omoth, Ty. *The Ultimate Collection of Pro Basketball Records.* Sports Illustrated Kids. North Mankato, Minn.: Capstone Press, 2013.

Internet Sites

FactHound offers a safe, fun way to find Internet sites related to this book. All of the sites on FactHound have been researched by our staff.

Here's all you do:

Visit *www.facthound.com*

Type in this code: 9781476561646

Super-cool stuff!

Check out projects, games and lots more at
www.capstonekids.com

Index

Allen, Ray, 20, 22, 23, 44
All-Star Games, 6, 7, 15, 18, 26, 27, 30, 31, 35, 39, 42, 43
Anthony, Carmelo, 37, 39, 45
Arizona State University, 30
Artesia High School, 30

Bird, Larry, 32, 34, 35, 45
Boston Celtics, 11, 22, 34
Bryant, Joe, 10
Bryant, Kobe, 8, 10, 44

Carter, Vince, 41, 43, 45
Charlotte Bobcats, 7
Charlotte Hornets, 10
Chicago Bulls, 6
Cleveland Cavaliers, 7, 18
Curry, Stephen, 21, 23, 44

Dallas Mavericks, 7
Davidson College, 23
Denver Nuggets, 39
Duke University, 18
Duncan, Tim, 13, 15, 44
Durant, Kevin, 36, 38, 42, 45

Erving, Julius, 43
Everett High School, 35

Garnett, Kevin, 22
Golden State Warriors, 23

Griffin, Blake, 40, 42, 45

Harden, James, 28, 30, 45

Indiana State University, 34, 35
Irving, Kyrie, 16, 18, 44

James, LeBron, 5, 7, 39, 44
Johnson, Magic, 33, 34, 35, 45
Jordan, Michael, 4, 6, 10, 44

Los Angeles Clippers, 26, 42
Los Angeles Lakers, 10, 11, 14, 35
Louisiana State University, 14

Mainland High School, 43
Marquette University, 31
Miami Heat, 7, 14, 22, 31
Michigan State University, 34, 35
Miller, Reggie, 22
Milwaukee Bucks, 11, 22
Minnesota Timberwolves, 19, 22
MVP awards, 7, 11, 14, 15, 18, 27, 31, 34, 35, 38, 45

NBA championships, 6, 7, 10, 11, 14, 15, 22, 27, 31, 34, 35, 44, 45
NCAA championships, 6, 11, 39
New Orleans Hornets, 26
New York Knicks, 39

Oklahoma City Thunder, 7, 30, 38
Oklahoma University, 42
O'Neal, Shaquille, 12, 14, 15, 44
Orlando Magic, 14

Parker, Tony, 25, 27, 45
Paul, Chris, 24, 26, 45
Pierce, Paul, 22

Robinson, David, 15
Rubio, Ricky, 17, 19, 44

San Antonio Spurs, 7, 15, 27
Seattle SuperSonics, 22, 38
Spanish ACB League, 19
Springs Valley High School, 34
St. Vincent-St. Mary High School, 7
Syracuse University, 39

Toronto Raptors, 43

University of Connecticut, 22
University of North Carolina, 6, 43
University of Texas, 38

Wade, Dwyane, 29, 31, 45
Wake Forest University, 15, 26
West, Jerry, 9, 11, 44
West Virginia University, 11

Library of Congress Cataloging-in-Publication Data

Forest, Christopher.
  Side-by-side basketball stars : comparing pro basketball's greatest players / by Christopher Forest.
    pages cm.—(Sports illustrated kids. Side-by-side sports.)
  Includes bibliographical references and index.
  Summary: "Compares the greatest pro basketball players in history"—Provided by publisher.
  ISBN 978-1-4765-6164-6 (library binding)
  ISBN 978-1-4765-6169-1 (paperback)
  1. Basketball players—Rating of—Juvenile literature. I. Title.
  GV884.A1F67 2015
  796.3230922—dc23   2014009745

Editorial Credits

Anthony Wacholtz, editor; Ted Williams, designer; Eric Gohl, media researcher; Gene Bentdahl, production specialist

Photo Credits

Newscom: Cal Sport Media/Chris Szagola, 17, Icon SMI/TSN, 9, MCT/Kyndell Harkness, 19; Sports Illustrated: Al Tielemans, 23, Andy Hayt, cover (bottom), 33, Bill Frakes, 14, 16, Bob Rosato, 41, Damian Strohmeyer, 22, 37, David E. Klutho, 15, 39, John Biever, 18, 44 (all), John D. Hanlon, 11, John W. McDonough, cover (top), 5, 7, 8, 10, 12, 13, 20, 21, 24, 25, 26, 27, 28, 29, 30, 31, 36, 38, 40, 42, 45 (all), Manny Millan, 4, 6, 32, 35, 43, Walter Iooss Jr., 34

Design Elements: Shutterstock